SRI LANKA

"Splendid Island"

Nance Lui Fyson

Dryad Press Limited   London

The Islands series

What have these people in common: Enid Blyton, Daniel Defoe, Robert Louis Stevenson and Roy Plomley? They have all written about islands, islands as places of adventure or fantasy. Think for a moment of the many stories or events that are associated with islands. What do you know about "Fortress Falklands", or Alcatraz, or the adventures of Robinson Crusoe? Islands have long held a special appeal and this series sets out to explore the fascination of islands.

Every island is unique, with a different location, a distinctive history and a particular personality. And yet about them all there are similarities, too. Island cultures are distinct because they are isolated, set apart from mainstream societies. They can be remote, places of refuge or sanctuary, where you can "get away from it all"! Monks and rich recluses have chosen island homes because they wanted seclusion. Other island inhabitants have had no choice in the matter because the isolation of islands also makes them ideal places for imprisonment or exile; Alcatraz and Elba certainly have that one thing in common.

In many cases, too, the remoteness of islands has meant that life for people, animals and plants has remained undisturbed by the progress and change of the mainlands. Forms and ways of life survive which elsewhere have become extinct, as is the case on the remote and beautiful islands of the Galapagos.

Another common feature of island life is that it can present similar problems of survival. Is there enough land to grow food and to keep animals? Is there an ample supply of water?

Why do islands become deserted?

Islands, therefore, can be places of challenge where you must learn to survive, fending for yourself on limited resources, or places of isolation and retreat where you dream about the good life – and listen to your desert island discs!

In each book of the series the author's purpose is to explore the uniqueness of a particular island and to convey the special appeal of the island. There is no common approach but in every case the island can be seen as a system in which a society is linked to its physical environment. An island culture can show clearly how the natural environment influences the ways people make a living. It also shows how people learn to modify or change that environment to make life better or more secure. This is very much a geographical view of islands, but the ideas and study skills used in the books are not limited to those of the geographer. The one controlling idea of the series is that islands are special places; small enough to know well and varied enough to illustrate the rich diversity of environments and lifestyles from all parts of the world. Islands can be places of social experiment or strategic importance, of simple survival or extravagance. Islands are the world in miniature.

John Bentley
Series editor

For details of other books in the Islands series, please write to Dryad Press Limited, 8 Cavendish Square, London W1M 0AJ.

Contents

For Gerald

ACKNOWLEDGMENTS

All the photographs, inside the book and on the front cover, are by Nance Lui Fyson. The maps and diagrams were drawn by R.F. Brien.

Title page photograph
Coconut palm trees are an important resource, with leaves, wood and coconuts all being used for many purposes.

© Nance Lui Fyson 1988
First published 1988

Typeset by Tek-Art Ltd, Kent
and printed and bound in Great Britain by
Richard Clay Ltd,
Chichester, Sussex
for the publishers Dryad Press Limited,
8 Cavendish Square, London W1M 0AJ

ISBN 0 8521 9729 0

1

"Splendid Island"

Landing in paradise

Lush green carpets of coconut palms lay below as the plane swooped down to land. Sunny air of 32°C (90°F) warmed our pale faces as we stepped out. It was January. How different from the Britain we had left nearly 13 hours before. No wonder "Sri Lanka" means literally "Splendid Island". What a paradise it is.

It is sometimes hard to remember that such a beautiful place is also one of the world's poorer countries. People earn, on average, less than a tenth (sometimes *much* less) than what people earn in the UK. Living is cheaper in some ways (for example, there is no heavy winter coat to buy!), but most people simply do "have" less. For the poorest there, it is a struggle just to survive and have enough to eat. But while Sri Lanka is a "poor" island, it is also "rich" in many ways. Warm, friendly smiles, delicate crafts, beautiful temples, stylish dancing – these types of wealth do not show in a country's gross national product (GNP). Sri Lanka and its people have a grace and charm

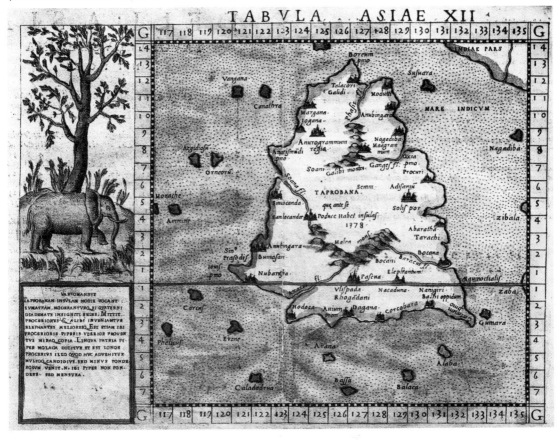

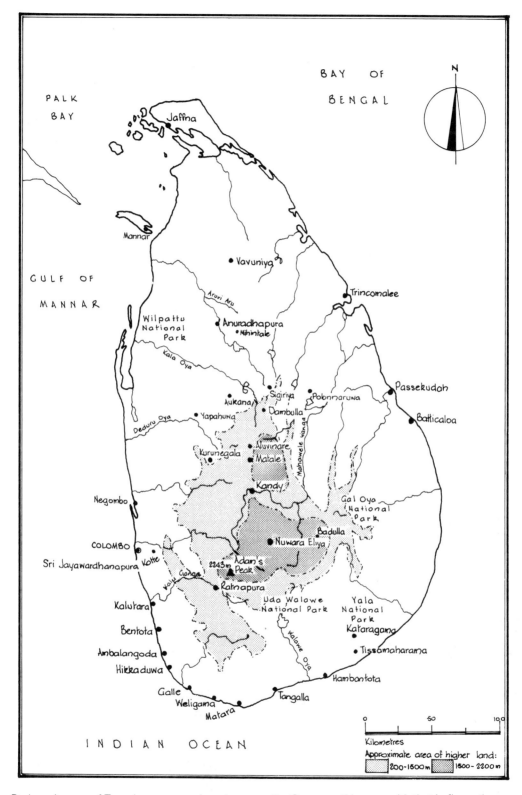

PALK
BAY

BAY OF
BENGAL

N

Jaffna

GULF OF
MANNAR

Mannar

• Vavuniya

Aruvi Aru

• Trincomalee

Wilpattu
National
Park

Kala Oya

• Anuradhapura
  • Mihintale

Passekudah

Deduru Oya

Aukana

Sigiriya

• Polonnaruwa

Dambulla

Batticaloa

• Yapahuwa

Mahaweli Ganga

Aluvihare

• Kurunegala

Matale

Kandy

Gal Oya
National
Park

Negombo

COLOMBO

Sri Jayawardhanapura

Kotte

Kelani Ganga

Badulla

Nuwara Eliya

2243m Adam's
        Peak

Ratnapura

Udo Walowe
National Park

Yala
National
Park

Kataragama

Kalutara

Bentota

Ambalangoda

Hikkaduwa

Galle

Weligama

Matara

Walowe Oya

Tissamaharama

Hambantota

Tangalla

INDIAN OCEAN

0   50   100

Kilometres

Approximate area of higher land:
200-1500m   1500-2200m

◄1 Ptolemy's map of Taprobane, second century
    A.D.

2 Compare this map with that in figure 1.

5

that countries much wealthier could envy.

A variety of names have been attached to the island throughout history. For the visitor today, there are still many different "Sri Lankas". The contrasts are part of what makes the island so fascinating. The modern, twentieth-century aspects mix with life much as it has been for hundreds of years.

What's in a name?

Britons and others have been attracted to this magical place for centuries. Romans called the island "Taprobane". Muslim traders described it as "Serendib". When the Portuguese arrived in the early sixteenth century they called it "Ceilao". Dutch explorers, who arrived in the seventeenth century, changed the name to "Ceylan". It was changed again to "Ceylon" by the British, who colonized the island from 1796.

The Sinhalese people, who make up 70% of the population, have always called their home "Lanka"; and for the Tamil people, 20% of the population, "Ilankai" has always been the name. Although the island became an independent country in 1948, it was not until 1972 that the colonial name of Ceylon was replaced by "Lanka". The added "Sri" means "resplendant" or "splendid".

"The Spice Isle"

Modern tourists come for the sun and the sights, but cinnamon was the tasty spice luring the Portuguese and Dutch centuries ago. Nearly all of the world's cinnamon still comes from a small area in the south-west of the island. The spice comes from branches, which must be peeled. Children often help with this work. Sticks of cinnamon are cut, dried, smoked and put together in bundles. The remains of the branches are used as firewood, and the leaves are taken to a distillery where they are steamed to make cinnamon oil. Many other spices are grown as well. Can the spices shown in figure 3 be grown in the UK?

3 Examples are shown and explained at a "Spice Garden", where spices are grown. Here is a list of some of the spices in the photo: cardamom, cloves, mustard, dill, anise, mace/nutmeg, cinnamon. Can you pick out which bowl contains which spice? (Answers on page 61.) How are these spices used?

4 Sri Lanka in relation to the rest of Asia.

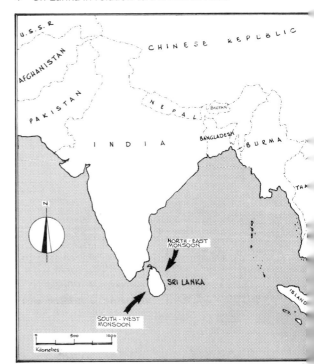

The Climate

Two different monsoons affect the island every year. Monsoons are high winds that come in certain seasons. The one on the south-west of Sri Lanka brings winds and rains to the southern and western coasts and central Hill Country within the months from May to September. From November to March it is the turn of the north-east to receive heavy rains and high winds. While one area is having a monsoon, the other side of the island is generally dry and sunny, although some brief showers do occur. Monsoons are sometimes called "trade winds". This is because ancient traders relied on the winds for sailing their ships.

Sri Lanka's tropical climate has warm to hot weather all year round. No snow has ever been recorded on the island, but temperatures vary, mainly according to elevation.

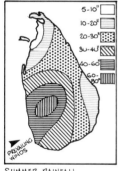

SUMMER RAINFALL
(MAY - OCT)

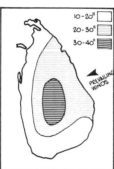

WINTER RAINFALL
(NOV - APR)

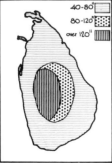

ANNUAL RAINFALL

5   Sri Lanka's rainfall pattern (generalized). The south-west corner of the island is known as the "Wet Zone", with adequate rainfall for farming. The rest of the island needs irrigation.

"Teardrop of India"

While known for centuries as "The Spice Isle", Sri Lanka has been called also the "teardrop of India". A look at figure 4 shows why. The island is only 48 km (30 miles) from India's south-east coast. Sri Lanka's greatest length is 435 km (270 miles) and greatest width is 225 km (140 miles). The total land area is a mere 65,610 sq km (25,332 sq miles). This is about the same area as Northern Ireland and Eire together, but today there are over 16 million people living in Sri Lanka – three times as many as in Northern Ireland and Eire. How might the population density affect the way that land is used and how people live?

"Land of Gems"

Another name Sri Lanka has had for centuries is "Land of Gems". The island is one of the five main gem-bearing countries of the world. Blue sapphires and rubies are the most valuable stones found, but there are also cat's eyes,

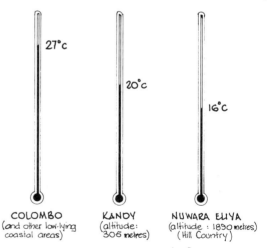

6   Average temperatures (for the whole year) in three different towns.

What general points could you make about how the temperature varies from the low coastal areas to the central Hill Country? How might this affect life in various parts of the island?

7 ‛A gem pit near Ratnapura. The illam *piled in the foreground is coarse, water-borne gravel that has been dug from below the earth. It must all be sifted through to find any gems.*
  What adjectives would you use to describe a gem pit? What adjectives would you use to describe the gems that are found and the jewellery made from them? Is there much of a contrast?

alexandrites, tourmalines, garnets and others.

Most gems are mined from pits where a mixture of gems are found together. The stones are in a coarse gravel, buried beneath a layer of clay. Miners dig through the clay to reach the gravel and bring it to the surface. The only machines used are for pumping water out of the pit. The gravel is then put in baskets which act as sieves. Men stand waist-high in water, rotating the baskets so that light soil is washed away. What is left is searched carefully by hand.

A less common, and less successful, way of gem-mining is by river-dredging. Bamboo sticks with special blades are used to collect gravel. This method is possible only in the dry season.

The main gem-bearing area is 101 km (63 miles) south-east of the city of Colombo. The place-name "Ratnapura" means literally "Town of Gems", and the world's first Gemmological Museum is located there. Find Ratnapura on the map, figure 2.

COCONUTS RULE OK!

What can you make from a coconut palm? (There are many different types.) Here is a list of some of the many clever uses seen in Sri Lanka:

- plait the leaves (about 400) into a roof for a house
- weave the leaves into a screen to shield a house from the road
- use the empty half-shells tied to rubber trees to collect the milky latex as it flows out
- use the empty half-shells as bowls to hold paint in art class, foods in a kitchen
- pile empty coconut shells as a permanent hedge/wall
- use empty coconut shells as fuel for a fire
- carve coconuts into monkeys and other shapes and sell these to tourists. (Shake and you can hear the milk is still inside.)
- use coconut tree wood
- cut open the bright orange King Coconut and drink the water
- use coconut oil for frying
- use coconut milk in cooking curries
- add coconut milk to a batter of rice flour to make cup-shaped pancakes called *appa* (hoppers)
- cook rice in coconut milk to make *kiribath* (milk rice)
- use dessicated coconut in side dishes, curries
- make coconut flour
- put coconut in dough with flour, water and salt to make *roti* (substitute for rice)
- use coconut to make sticky rich sweets
- use grated coconut plus red pepper, onions, lime, salt and slivers of fish to make *pol sambol*
- process coconut into copra (the dried kernel of the nut) for cooking oil
- make *thelijja*, non-alcoholic drink from coconut sap (toddy)
- make *arrack*, fermented alcoholic drink from coconut sap (toddy)

- braid coir fibre from inside shell to make ropes, carpets and nets
- use brown coir fibre to make brushes and brooms, for packing, stuffing furniture, and for insulation

The coconut palm is even important when someone dies. Strings of knotted palm fronds (*gokkola*) are hung across a road for a funeral. *Gokkola* are used for other processions as well.

Can you think of any more uses?

8   Leaves for roofing, screens, mats . . . . In many poorer countries like Sri Lanka, thatched-roof homes are now mainly lived in by low-income families. There are also more "modern" homes made of brick and cement blocks with clay-tile roofs – but these cost more. In your country, are there homes with thatched roofs? What is used to make the thatch? Is it mainly poorer or richer people in your country who live in thatched-roof houses today? Was this so 150 years ago?

9   Grated coconut for foods . . . . A woman prepares a curry in her rural home kitchen. (The cooking fire is in the top left corner.) This is typical of poorer homes on the island. How does it compare with kitchens in homes in your country?
▼

▲
10   Brown coir fibre for carpets . . . .

11   Here a coconut shell is being used to collect latex from a rubber tree. This is called "tapping". Trees can be tapped as often as twice a week for ten months of the year. Slanting cuts are made in the trunk and the milky latex flows out. The latex collected in the shells is emptied into buckets and taken to a rubber factory. Here it is strained and water is added. The mixture is then dried and rolled through ringers, making sheets and mats.

Rubber tree seedlings were first brought to the island in 1876, by the British. A British agent had smuggled rubber seeds out of Brazil, and these were cultivated in Kew Gardens, London. Some of the seedlings were then taken to Sri Lanka, to become the first rubber trees in Asia. Which other countries in South-East Asia now produce a lot of natural rubber?

"The Coconut Isle"

Another name for Sri Lanka might almost be "The Coconut Isle". About 2½ thousand million coconuts are produced each year. Some products from these, like the coir fibre inside the shell, are important exports. The coconut palms grow all over coastal areas, except in parts of the far north, where the palmyrah palm is more common. How do you reach coconuts (which are at the top of the tree)? Sri Lankans either use a long stick with a knife attached, or climb up and bring the coconuts down.

Changing island

At the time of independence in 1948, Sri Lanka was a typical colonial economy. Only a few primary products (tea, rubber, coconuts) made up 97% of the island's earnings from exports, and nearly one third of all workers relied on these products for jobs. Most of what the country earned from these exports was used to buy manufactured goods.

In the late 1950s, tea and rubber prices began to decline. The island was earning less and less from its few exports. An effort was made to manufacture more goods in Sri Lanka so that fewer imports would be needed. (A number of other poorer, ex-colonial countries have faced a similar problem.)

A new government took office in 1977 and major changes were made. An "open economic policy" began, encouraging foreign investors to create more industry on the island.

12 Sri Lanka is like many other poorer countries in having a large part of the workforce in farming. But Sri Lanka (and many other poorer countries) are increasing their industry. What are the advantages to Sri Lanka of the change shown by these diagrams?

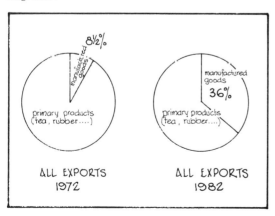

ALL EXPORTS 1972 ALL EXPORTS 1982

Exports and imports

The island's main exports have been changing for nearly the last 200 years. The British brought in coffee as a plantation crop in the 1830s, and coffee soon replaced cinnamon as the main export crop. A leaf disease then developed, ruining many coffee trees, and in the 1870s tea began to become more important.

From figures 13 and 14, what is now the single most important export of the island? Which country is the single most important customer of Sri Lanka? In the early 1980s, what was the single most important import of the island? Which country is the single most important seller to Sri Lanka? What general points could you make comparing the main exports and imports of Sri Lanka?

13 Main exports (1982) (by value).

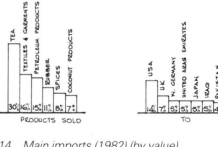

14 Main imports (1982) (by value).

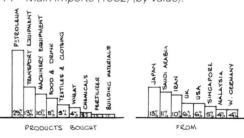

(Source: *Lloyds Bank Group Economic Report, 1984*)

Sri Lanka's first "Free Trade Zone" was established in 1978, producing goods to export, and a few more zones have been created since then. Over 47 industries, mainly producing garments and electronic goods, operate in these zones. The foreign firms which own the factories have several tax and other advantages from the Sri Lankan government. They also have the advantage of being able to pay workers much less than they would have to pay workers in their *own* country. About 80% of workers in the island's Free Trade Zones are young women.

Sri Lanka is still not heavily industrial, but you can see from figure 12 that industry is growing. How have manufactured goods increased as a percentage of all exports? In the early 1980s, fewer than 15% of workers were employed in industry – but this too is growing. About one third of manufacturing is processing agricultural products. More processing into finished products on the island means more jobs and earnings for Sri Lankans. For example, most rubber is exported in raw bales to other countries – but in the 1980s Sri Lanka began itself to produce tyres and some other rubber goods.

Outside the Free Trade Zones, most manufacturing is publicly owned. Products include cement, paper, plywoods, chemicals, ceramics, leather goods, oils and fats, textiles, hardware, steel and fertilizers. Government training centres offer courses to help people develop skills needed for industry. Besides larger factories, there are also some small-scale industries. An example is a food-processing centre which began in 1982. This provides jobs for young people in the village. Locally produced fruits and vegetables are made into such products as jams and fruit juices.

Meanwhile, farming is still the main occupation for over half of Sri Lanka's workers.

There are changes here too. *Chena* (slash-and-burn) is an old method of farming used on flatter, lower land. The farmer sets fire to an area of forest during the dry season, and then crops are planted on the cleared land, including cucumber, brinjal (long egg-plant), water-melon, pumpkin, tomato, climbing beans, mung beans and gourds. Maize (corn) and chillies may be grown as well. Once the crops have been harvested, the farmers move to another area and clear that. *Chena* has had bad environmental effects: forests have been used up and the topsoil has become poorer as nutrients have been taken from the land by farming. The government now discourages *chena* and is helping farmers to learn better techniques.

Some new crops are being introduced to the island, such as the soya bean. These beans have a high protein content and are a good food to provide better nourishment for the people. A factory making soya milk was opened in the early 1980s.

Social changes also are taking place in Sri Lanka. As industries grow in the Free Trade Zones, some girls move away from home to live near the factories. Some workers are migrating to other countries to work for a few years. They return with savings, and new experiences of the world. Shops sell cassettes of Western music, and television shows programmes from Europe and America. Tourists coming to the island are another influence. Your Sri Lankan guide to an ancient site today might be wearing "Super Star" trainer shoes. . .

"The Variety Isle"

For all its many names, Sri Lanka might really best be called "The Variety Isle". At the end of one long day full of surprises, our tour driver said: "Now, everything of interest has stopped." But that was only until tomorrow. . .

2

Ancient sites and Buddhism

An ancient civilization

The exports of Sri Lanka show very clearly that European colonial powers have left their mark on the island. However, this has been only in the last few hundred years of history. The culture of this splendid island goes back *thousands* of years. Centuries before the birth of Christ, Sri Lanka's civilization was highly advanced. Part of what makes the country interesting today are the remains of this ancient past. These are a popular attraction to tourists and therefore also a help to the economy.

The ancient cities were in the "dry zone" of Sri Lanka (areas short of water for farming). There were large-scale irrigation networks as early as the first century A.D. By the sixth century these reservoirs (called *wewas*) were throughout the dry zone. Their construction shows clever engineering, worthy of a great civilization. Thousands of reservoirs still dot these lowland areas, and most are stocked with fish.

Anuradhapura

Some ancient remains are linked to the religion, Buddhism, now followed by about 70% of Sri Lanka's people. Anuradhapura, the most important of the ancient towns, is an example. Human settlement began there in about 500 B.C., and it was the capital of Sri Lanka for about 1400 years, until the tenth century A.D. Buddhism was introduced to the island at Anuradhapura in the third century B.C.

The most sacred place in the town is the Bo tree – the oldest documented tree on earth. It was grown from a sapling of the tree under which Gautama Buddha (the founder of Buddhism) had become "enlightened". The "Brazen Palace", which stands next to the Bo tree, was built originally as a monk's residence, in the second century B.C. The palace is named after the copper which once covered the roof.

Siddhartha Gautama was a prince living in the sixth and fifth centuries B.C., in what is now northern India. He left palace life at the age of 29 to look for an end to human suffering, and while meditating under a tree he discovered the "Middle Way". This means a lifestyle avoiding extreme pleasure and pain. Gautama said we suffer because of our attachments to people and things in an ever-changing world. We can lose our desire (and suffering) by wisdom, morality and mental discipline.

There are now varying ideas of Buddhism. In the Mahayana school, the Buddha is an all-powerful god who can be asked for help in your life. In Sri Lankan "Theravada" Buddhism, the Buddha is seen as an enlightened man but not as a god. There are, however, deities that are prayed to – especially in times of family crisis, drought or other problems.

Positions of the Buddha

Buddhists pray at the Bo tree, and at huge temples (*pansalas*) old and new. There are also small shrines across the island, often by the side of the road. People stop, make their coin offerings and say prayers.

At the temples and shrines the Buddha is in

different sitting and reclining positions – all of which have a meaning. Even hand and foot positions are important. For example, if the reclining Buddha's feet are in line together, this means that the Buddha is at rest. If one foot is in front, the Buddha is dead. In figure 15, is the Buddha on the right "just resting" or "dead"?

The Five Precepts (Rules)

Devout Buddhists are expected to follow the "Five Precepts". This means no killing, stealing, lying, sexual misconduct, or drinking of intoxicating liquor. On *poya* days, linked to phases of the moon, a devout follower is expected to not eat after noon. On these days Buddhists should also not sit on comfortable seats, or witness music and dance (these are "pleasures of the senses"). Monks, in their simple orange robes, have a few extra rules to follow on *poya* days. They should not wear beautifying adornments and should not touch money of any kind.

As with all religions, people vary in how devout they are. Not everyone follows all the rules. However, the four *poya* days each month are considered important by most people. Buddhists visit the *pansalas* and offer trays of flowers. Small oil-lamps are lit and incense is burned. *Poya* day ceremonies include sermons

15 Buddhas old . . . . The Gal Vihara (meaning "rock shrine") at Polonnaruwa. There are four twelfth-century statues cut from a single granite wall. The standing Buddha (seven metres high) is in a rare cross-armed pose. The reclining Buddha is 14 metres long

16 . . . and new. This modern temple at Matale was built in the early 1900s. The Buddha here is the largest in Sri Lanka. About 50 monks live at the temple and over 20,000 pictures about the life of Buddha decorate the temple walls. Shoes and head-coverings must be removed at Buddhist sites and temples (whether you are praying or not). Which religion asks you to cover your head in church? For Buddhists, white is the colour of death. White flags line the road for a funeral procession. What colour is associated with death in your country?

as well. Visitors may see hotel signs saying "*Poya* day. No alcoholic drinks today". Full moon *poya* days are the most important and are national holidays. Schools are closed if these happen on a Monday to Friday.

Earning "merit"

Like all religions, Buddhism is very complex. There are also different kinds, with somewhat different beliefs. An important basic belief of Buddhism is that we are trapped in an endless cycle of *samsara* (re-birth). People must work to improve their chances for a better life when they are re-born. Showing compassion and being of service to others are two ways by which someone can hope to make his or her next life on earth better than the present one. This is only part of why visitors to Sri Lanka can experience much warmth and hospitality from local people.

17   Temple of the Tooth, Kandy. Calling people to prayer. How do other religions summon people to prayer and worship?

Dagobas

Although Gautama Buddha lived many centuries ago, there are buildings on the island thought to hold some of his remains. For Sri Lankans these are sacred places.

"*Dagoba*" is the word for a Buddhist religious monument thought to contain a relic of the Buddha. Around Anuradhapura there are three great *dagoba* half-spheres. Thuparama Dagoba, built in the third century B.C., is believed to hold the Buddha's collarbone. Nearby is the Ruvanvelisaya Dagoba (second century B.C.), which is surrounded by a wall of 336 painted stone elephants standing shoulder-to-shoulder. Jetawana Dagoba is Anuradhapura's largest temple.

Temple of the Tooth

The most important relic of the Buddha is said to be in Kandy. This great treasure, the Buddha's left eyetooth, came to Sri Lanka early in the fourth century A.D. and has been kept in Kandy since 1590. It is so valued that wars have been fought to possess it. A replica is paraded through the streets of Kandy for two weeks every August, in the city's main festival.

The Tooth Relic itself is said to be kept in the "Temple of the Tooth". Visitors and worshippers flock to this remarkable place, which is open from dawn to dusk. *Pujas* (times of religious offerings) are held at dawn (about 6 a.m.), mid-morning (about 11 a.m.) and dusk (about 6.30 p.m.) and during these times visitors queue to file past and "view" the relic. But the tooth itself is not visible: it is contained within seven caskets of gold of increasing size. These caskets are ornamented with precious gems.

Other treasures within the Temple – doors of silver and ivory, painted ceilings and woodcarvings – all make a visit there a visual treat. Excited drums and horns calling worshippers during *pujas* heighten the emotional feeling. The "tooth", and the Bo tree in Anuradhapura, are very important to Buddhists in Sri Lanka.

Temple of Dambulla

As well as temple buildings, Sri Lanka also has some ancient cave temples. Most impressive

18   Part of a carving on an old building at
Polonnaruwa. What in the photo suggests that the
carver had a sense of humour?

19   Remains of the heart of the ancient city at
Polonnaruwa. The semi-circular slab of decorated
granite on the ground is called a "moonstone".

is the series of caves at the village of Dambulla. These date from the second century B.C. The tour by torchlight reveals remarkable statues and paintings, many from the twelfth century A.D. and earlier.

Polonnaruwa

In the eleventh century A.D., the capital of Sri Lanka was shifted south from Anuradhapura to Polonnaruwa for about two hundred years. The Cholas of India, who invaded and ruled Sri Lanka for 75 years, chose Polonnaruwa because there were fewer mosquitoes causing malaria and the site was easier to defend. The monuments here are in better repair and somewhat more complete than at Anuradhapura. The heart of ancient Polonnaruwa was a group of twelve buildings, known today as the "Quadrangle".

Remains of the old city are being restored, with the help of the United Nations' UNESCO Cultural Triangle Project. There is a Ministry of Cultural Affairs' yellow box outside many sites, encouraging visitors to donate. These say "Help the Cultural Triangle to Save Monuments".

Moonstones

Moonstones (see fig. 19) are a common form of ancient sculpture on the island. The bands of carved decoration vary, but all have special meanings. Animals are often included. The elephant is a symbol of "birth", the bull a symbol of "decay", the lion represents "disease" and the horse symbolizes "death". "Geese" represent the difference between good and evil. At the centre of many moonstones is the lotus petal. The lotus is a sacred flower to Buddhists. What symbols do you have in your culture for ideas like "death"?

Sigiriya Rock

Not all of Sri Lanka's ancient sites are linked to Buddhism. Sigiriya (see-gih-REE-yah) is a massive redstone monolith which once held a royal palace high in the sky. (See figure 42 on page 38.) In the fifth century A.D. King Kasyapa erected his royal buildings on top of a huge rock mountain. Hundreds of paintings of lovely maidens adorned the stones leading to the top. Only twenty-two of these fresco paintings can be seen today.

It seems rather odd to build a royal residence on top of a huge rock. But then, Kasyapa was no ordinary ruler. He was the first son of King Dhatusena of Anuradhapura. Kasyapa feared that his younger half-brother would become king. This half-brother had a mother of royal blood, while Kasyapa's mother was a commoner. Because of his fear, Kasyapa took the throne and walled up his father alive in a tomb. The half-brother fled to India. A mixture of fear and arrogance prompted Kasyapa to build his palace in the sky. Some years later his half-brother returned with troops. In the battle, Kasyapa ended up cutting his own throat. The brother became king and moved the palace back to Anuradhapura, but Sigiriya was not forgotten. Sight-seers have been visiting the rock and seeing remains of the ancient palace for hundreds of years.

One of the strangest features of the site is the "Mirror Wall" which was coated with lime. It still reflects like glass today. Visitors to the site over a thousand years ago carved comments and poems in this wall. Visitors today can see what must be Sri Lanka's very oldest graffiti!

3

Getting around

Road travel

To see the ancient sites (and other sights), driving around the island is best. Hiring a car with driver is actually cheaper than hiring a car for self-drive. It is also infinitely wiser. Motoring is a wonderful but hair-raising experience in Sri Lanka. The roads are full of wandering children, bicycles, cows, water-buffalo, dogs – as well as many holes. Wild elephants may pose problems as well. A Sri Lankan driver is a master of the swerve and frequently uses the car horn!

Driving at night is even more of a test, as none of the wandering people, animals or bicycles bears any lights! (One exceptional bicyclist was seen holding a hand torch.) Street lighting exists in some areas, but is missing in much of the countryside. Villages at night are often eerily lit by open shop-fronts with kerosene lamps, bare bulbs and sometimes fluorescent strips.

The car driver shares the road with vehicles carrying some spectacular loads. Ox-drawn

20   *A bicycle balances a load of bright orange King Coconuts. These are cut open and the water inside is drunk straight from the shell. (Because tap and well water on the island is impure and must be boiled before drinking, coconuts are popular sources of safe refreshment.) The sign at the left says "Motor Bus Halting Place". Buses and mini-buses are another way to move around.*

21　An ox-drawn cart. Vehicles like this have not changed for centuries. What problems would a car driver have sharing the road with carts and bicycles carrying big loads?

carts (straight out of the seventeenth if not the fifth century) lumber slowly by, laden with firewood, harvested rice, or heaps of coconut coir for making into ropes, nets and mats. The loads on bicycles are even more amazing. Large water jars, sacks of grain, strings of coconuts, loads of firewood, huge boxes are balanced with impressive skill. Just when you think you have seen everything possible, a bicycle rides by with whole sharks strapped on! (See the photograph on the front cover.) Bicycles are an important means of transport in Sri Lanka. As Sri Lanka is one of the world's poorest countries, not many people can afford to own a car.

There are also lorries, government buses, private mini-buses, motorbikes, and, in Colombo, the main city, and Galle, one historic city, three-wheeled pedicabs called "trishaws". These carry two passengers and are cheaper to hire than taxis.

For those travelling by bus, signs indicate a "Motor Bus Halting Place", or in some areas there is simply "!" followed by the silhouette of a bus.

Road surfaces vary on the island but maintenance can be very poor. Sometimes clay is used to fill holes in the road, and this is washed out by the next rain. There are no motorways in Sri Lanka. When observed, the speed limit in towns and built-up areas is 30 m.p.h., and 40 m.p.h. elsewhere.

Sri Lanka is an assault on the senses. Motoring offers a panorama of visual delights as you whizz along. There is also sometimes the feeling that you are taking your life in your hands. As one Sri Lankan newspaper commented in 1985: "Today the roads have become one of the most menacing arenas of national life. The proliferation of vehicles of every variety, compounded by the recklessness of many drivers who take to the roads, has contributed to the high incidence of road accidents." The words "fully insured" can be seen on the back of some vans.

The government announced in 1985 that Sri Lanka's 150 driving schools were finally to be regulated by law. Good drivers must have

greeted this news with some relief. Anything which adds more safety without taking away the appealing adventure of motoring on the island is to be welcomed by tourists and locals alike.

Railways

Trains still serve a number of key towns, but the railways have been in decline in recent years. Imports of cars, lorries, buses and mini-buses have meant increasing alternatives for both passengers and freight. Also, many railways now offer only a 2nd or 3rd class service. First-class means an air-conditioned coach, observation saloon or sleeper berth.

Railways lines between Colombo, the main city on the coast, and inland Kandy, an important cultural centre, are long-standing.

22 & 23 Are more towns on the island reached by roads or by railways? The railways, built in colonial times, show a pattern typical of many countries that have been colonies. The rail lines lead out to the main ports on the coasts. Why is this so? What main product is transported from the area around Nuwara Eliya and Badulla to Colombo?

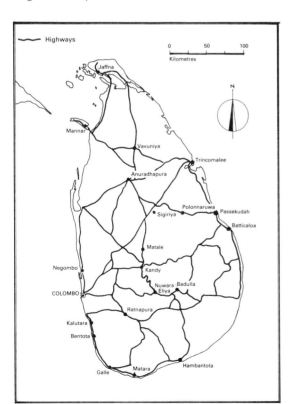

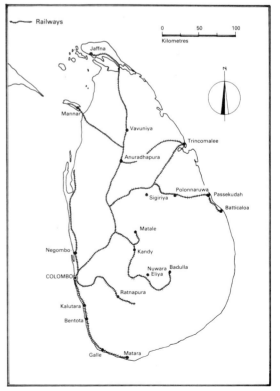

24 A Sri Lankan train. How does this compare with the way trains look in your country?

25 The percentage of people living in towns in Sri Lanka and the UK. Which country has more of its people living in towns and cities? Suppose you were in charge of improving transport in Sri Lanka. What kinds of transport would you emphasize? How might the high proportion living in rural areas affect what you decide?

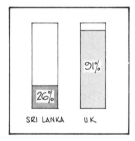

They began in 1867. The current daily express between the two cities is still very popular and seats must be booked well in advance. Piped-in music is an unusual feature of the restaurant car.

Trains do still lure the tourists as well as locals. The Ceylon Government Railway offers tours of the island lasting from one to six days. These use luxury air-conditioned coaches, include meals and lodging, and cover all transfers between hotels.

Road signs near railway lines still show an old-fashioned silhouette of a puffing steam train. Diesel trains are in general use, but the government is considering re-introducing some real steam trains as a tourist feature. The example of Britain's steam trains has been noted in the Sri Lankan newspapers.

Trains are generally slow-moving in Sri Lanka. Often locals sit on the line chatting, getting up only to let a train through – and then resuming their place. Another unnerving sight to visitors is people calmly walking along a railway line, carrying loads on their heads the shortest way from A to B.

Language

You can always "get around" in Sri Lanka with English, which is widely spoken and understood, although less so in rural areas. (Why do you think this is so?) English was in fact the official language until 1958, when Sinhala became official. The Tamil minority speaks Tamil, as well as English.

Place-names are simpler if you realize that "pura" or "puram" means town (i.e. Ratnapura = "town of gems"). "Nuwara" means "city", while "gama" in a place-name means "village". "Gala" or "giri" means "rock" or "hill". A name like Tissamaharama seems difficult – but, broken down into parts, it is simply "King Tissa's great park".

One word of Sinhala very useful to know is "āyoubōwan". This means literally "may you live long" – but is also good for "hello", "goodbye", and "how are you?"

Visitors to Sri Lanka find that, as in India, a waggle of the head from side to side means "yes" instead of "no"!

English	Sinhalese	Tamil
Hello (to a man)	Mahatmaya	Aiya
Hello (to a lady)	Nona mahatmaya	Thirumadhi
Please	Karunakara	Thayavu sai du
Thank you	Es-thu-ti	Nandri
Yes	Ov	Ahm
No	Na-tha (nay-hay)	Illai
My name is	Mage nama	Ennudaya payar

4
Wildlife and nature protection

A ride through Yala Game Park

"Three leopards! You are very lucky." Our guide at Ruhuna National Park was excited at the sighting. German and British tourists in the mini-van jostled for camera positions. A few hours' bumpy riding through the park (more popularly known as Yala) revealed a small sampling of the island's rich and varied wildlife. Spotted deer, crocodiles, peacocks, pelicans and jungle fowl were on view. Dangerous wild black buffalo and white buffalo stared back at us from shallow pools. A goup of five wild

elephants of varying sizes lumbered by. "Stay in your vehicle!" warned a skull and crossbones sign.

Protection of wildlife

Yala and another main national park called Wilpattu together hold much of the country's wildlife. Both parks (and others) were opened in 1938, after a Fauna and Flora Protection Ordinance was declared in 1937. Concern for wildlife is actually a very old tradition in Sri Lanka — recorded in even a twelfth-century royal transcript. Now, one-tenth of the island's land area is controlled by the Department of Wildlife Conservation.

There are various threats to wildlife. As a country develops, with more urban areas and industries, land and animal life are affected. There are also more specific threats. Some animals are hunted for their fur and tusks, which the poachers can sell to make money. What conflict can you see between economically developing the country and preserving wildlife?

Wildlife sanctuaries

Government wildlife sanctuaries are of several kinds. "Strict Natural Reserves" are for animals only and no visitors are allowed. (Scientific expeditions are permitted.) "Natural Reserves" admit some people but are mainly

26 *The main National Parks. Why would it be difficult to create more parks in a small island like Sri Lanka?*

to protect animal and bird life. The National Parks are for visitors, allowing them to see animals in their natural surroundings. The parks are increasingly popular with locals as well as tourists. All visitors to Yala numbered only about 3,000 in 1950 but were over 100,000 by 1980.

The two largest National Parks have small bungalows where visitors can stay overnight. Most are for Sri Lankans, but two in each park can be used by tourists. Basic living facilities (bedlinen, cutlery, crockery) are provided. Visitors bring their own food which is then prepared by the bungalow keeper and his assistant. Kerosene lamps are used for lighting, as in much of rural Sri Lanka.

27   A black buffalo at Yala Game Park wallows in a shallow pool. Are there any game parks in your country where you can drive through and see wild animals – lions? leopards? crocodiles? . . .

Wilpattu National Park is in the north-west of the island. The name comes from the many *villus* or small lakes. The land is mainly thick forest and includes about 270 km of jeep track. Tours are given in jeeps or in a mini-bus, with a tracker guide. The park is most famous for its leopards and sloth bears. In fact, we saw just one leopard there, crossing a road. More on view were crocodiles, iguanas and birds.

Wildlife at Yala is similar to that at Wilpattu, but Yala is especially known for its 100-200 wild elephants. The thorny scrub forest of semi-arid Yala is similar to the African bush environment.

By the ticket office at Yala there is an exhibition in glass cases. It shows examples of endangered species, such as the Star Tortoise. This is one of the most beautiful tortoises in the world and was common in the Dry Zone until recently.

The Yala exhibition also tells visitors that Sri Lanka has recorded 66 species of landsnakes. Nineteen of these are found only on the island and nowhere else in the world. Why do you think this is so? Of these landsnakes, only 13 have any large amount of venom and only five are deadly poisonous. Most of the snakes are harmless and even helpful to man. They play an important part in the balance of life between species. Snakes destroy rats, frogs and toads and in this way are very useful for keeping down the numbers of these pests. Can you construct a food chain with the snake in the middle of the chain?

Game laws and poaching

The problem of declining numbers of some species has led to several laws being passed. Sri Lanka's game laws are very strict. The following are either totally protected or cannot be legally hunted or killed:

* all birds, with the exception of a few considered harmful (e.g. the crow)
* most mammals, including leopards and all other cats, elephants, all deer, bear and buffalo
* crocodiles, water monitors (iguanas), all sea turtles, the Star Tortoise

28 *A Sri Lankan mother shows her child the exhibition at Yala Game Park. The entrance fee for the Park is much lower for Sri Lankans than for tourists. Is this a good idea? Do we/should we charge entry fees to National Parks in Britain? How could the money be used?*

for purposes directly related to conservation.

Private organizations

Besides government action, there are also private bird clubs and nature conservation organizations. The Wild Life and Nature Protection Society of Ceylon is the most active. Founded in 1894, the Society now has over 4000 members. It tries to lessen damage to the environment and one of its campaigns aims to save tropical rainforest. In the mid-1970s nearly 40% of the Dry Zone was under forest. By the mid-1980s this was only 20% and becoming less every day. People cutting down wood to use for fuel is one main reason for declining forests.

The Society is also worried about endangered species. The number of sea turtles is rapidly declining, partly because of over-fishing. One successful programme by the Society has been to set up turtle hatcheries in coastal areas. At Kosgoda, fishermen bring turtle eggs that have been left uncovered around the coast to a turtle hatchery. Many thousands of turtles have been safely hatched and released. Over-fishing is affecting such creatures as lobsters as well.

Animals valued

It is also illegal to transport skins or carcasses without a permit.

Poaching (hunting and killing animals illegally) is still a problem. The leopard is the most common target, hunted for its fur. Poisoned meat may be used to bait the cat, so that the fur remains unmarked by gunshot wounds. Game guards are doing what they can to arrest offenders. The Department of Wildlife Conservation does not have the vehicles needed to patrol all the land.

The government has taken a number of steps against threats to wildlife. Some important laws were introduced with the Wildlife Preservation Fund, set up by Sri Lanka's Parliament in 1960. Public donations can be made to the Fund and the money is used

Seeing wildlife in Sri Lanka is certainly not limited to the parks. A drive around the island is full of animal as well as human surprises: there are more than 400 species of birds; two types of monkey appear at the roadside and perched on signs. The grey langur with a dark face is considered quite shy. Red monkeys (the macaque) are brownish with a pink face and they can have a bad temper.

Animals such as oxen and water-buffalo are still much used for work in Sri Lanka – for instance, pulling carts and ploughs. Fortunately, *wild* creatures are valued by most Sri Lankans as much as work animals. Like people the world over, Sri Lankans also enjoy animals as pets. Dogs and cats are plentiful – eating rice and curry just like their owners!

Elephants

Two thousand wild elephants roam the Sri Lankan island. These are the Asian variety, which are much smaller than those found in Africa. They have a sweet tooth and like eating sugar-cane (and other crops) from fields. Farmers often spend nights in raised huts in the fields, making noises to frighten off the elephants and other pests.

Besides wild elephants, there are also about 500 tame elephants. These curl their trunks around logs and other loads and help lift and move. *Mahouts* (elephant masters) can be seen walking elephants along the road. Bells on the elephant jangle to warn motorists.

Elephants are decorated with colourful fabrics for festivals and processions. The elephant shape is everywhere – even small wooden ones are attached to some hotel room keys. The most popular brand of soft drinks on the island (bought at stands called "Cool Spots" or "Thirst Aid Stations") is called "Elephant House". Elephants are painted on to designs on cloth, tapped into patterns on brass, and appear in decorations on buildings, columns and signs.

Many elephants have been killed over the years so that the ivory in their tusks can be used for jewellery and carvings. In the 1960s it was realized that the whole species was in danger. A "Save the Elephant Fund" began worldwide in 1982. It became unlawful in Sri Lanka to use new ivory on jewellery or other items.

Some small ivory items are still being sold and it is estimated that worldwide some 70,000 elephants are being killed illegally each year.

29 Mahout *with a tame, working elephant. What animals are "working" animals in your country? Were there fewer or more working animals in your country 150 years ago?*

5

A taste of Sri Lanka

Rice and curry

If you asked Sri Lankans what is their basic dish, they would say quite simply "rice and curry". This means really a plateful of rice with helpings of different curries – and often some *sambol* and other extras. *Sambol* is a mixture of grated coconut, pickles, onions, lemon juice and sometimes dried fish. Red pepper makes this hot and spicy – "dynamite", as one Sri Lankan said with a smile.

The word "curry" comes from the Tamil word "*kari*", which simply means "sauce". The sauce for Sri Lankan curries is made from coconut milk. The white of the coconut is grated and mixed with a little water and then the mixture is squeezed. The milk may either be used thick or be squeezed with more water to make it thin. Vegetables, and sometimes either fish or meat, are cooked in the milk. A sour fish curry (*ambul thiyal*) made with tuna is one popular dish on the south of the island.

Curry powder adds flavouring to the dish. This is generally home-made, using a variety of local spices. One recipe mixes together fennel seed, coriander, cumin, tumeric, black and red pepper, mustard, cardamom, cloves, curry leaves and bay leaves, cinnamon and fenugreek. Another uses a mix of just coriander, cumin, anise seeds and curry leaves. Using chilli makes the curry taste "hot". A "white" curry is the mildest, without chilli. "Black" curry is a speciality of Sri Lanka. The colour comes from the roasted cumin seeds.

Rice is the main cereal grain. It supplies about 42% of all the calories Sri Lankans eat, and takes up about 40% of all farming land. There are about 15 varieties grown. Most popular on the island is a round-grain rice, different from the long-grain rice favoured in India. "Paddy" is unhusked rice which is planted to produce more rice. The paddy is sown in nursery fields until small plants grow, and then the seedlings are replanted in the

papadum (large fried wafers)

potato badum

leeks tempered

cabbage mustard curry

beef curry

rice (with slivers of carrot and onion)

30   Which plate in this photograph holds little "extras" to accompany the meal? Have you eaten any food similar to this? If so, try to describe the taste. (Eating some grated coconut helps to cool the mouth when eating hot curries.)

25

with tumeric, cinnamon, cloves and cardamom.

A dish called *kiribath* (rice cooked in coconut milk) is traditional for breakfast on New Year's Day and on the first day of each month. It is often eaten with a hot *sambol*. *Lamprai* is a curried snack. To make this, a mixture of rice boiled in bouillon and a dry curry is wrapped in a banana leaf and baked.

Pittu, roti and "hoppers"

Although rice is the main filler served with curries, one alternative is called *pittu*. Rice flour, coconut and water are mixed into small dry lumps, which are packed into a bamboo mould and steamed. Tubes of *pittu* are served warm with curries.

Roti is another substitute for rice eaten with curries. The flatbread is made from dough (flour, coconut, water and a little salt).

"Hoppers" (*appa*) are thin, cup-shaped pancakes made from a batter of rice flour and coconut milk. A spoonful of batter is poured into a deep curved iron dish (like a small wok) which is then rotated over a fire. The hoppers cook quickly and come out crispy on the outside and soft within. Besides plain hoppers, there are egg hoppers (*bithara*), with an egg cooked in the centre, and other types.

Sri Lankans traditionally eat using the fingers of the right hand. Rice hoppers, *pittu* and *roti* can all be used to mop up the sauces of curries.

"Stringhoppers" (*indiappa*) are made by squeezing rice flour dough through a sieve, to make small strings. These are steamed on small woven trays, one tray on top of another over a low fire.

Spices and Ayurvedic medicine

Spices are used for medicine as well as food in Sri Lanka. Ginger and coriander boiled together in tea offer delicious comfort for colds. Cloves are used to relieve toothache — as is oil from the cinnamon tree. The use of spices and other plants is part of the island's traditional "Ayurvedic" medicine. Many herbs and other

31   The man is on his way to the rice field where the woman in the background is already working. Growing rice in this kind of water-logged field is called "wet paddy" or "swamp rice". (Rice can be grown in an ordinary field as well.) The man is carrying a simple digging stick to help him work. Curved-blade hand tools called "sickles" will be used to harvest the plants. How does this compare with how farmers grow crops in Britain? What big machines are used on farms in the UK?

main fields. There are two main rice crops each year on the island. The main *maha* crop is sown in August-September and harvested in February-March. A supplementary *yala* crop is sown in May. Rice-growing has hardly changed on the island over the centuries. In a few areas, tractors are now being used instead of water-buffalo.

Rice may be served either boiled plain white, or an attractive yellow shade. This yellow rice has been cooked in coconut milk and flavoured

32 What popular Italian food looks like the stringhoppers in this photograph? Note: the Italian *food is made from* wheat *flour. Stringhoppers are made from* rice *flour.*

plants are grown especially to use in curing.

In Sri Lanka and parts of India the spice tumeric is known as "saffron" because of its yellow colour. It kills bacteria in food and from ancient times has been used as a disinfectant, put on wounds. Tourists sometimes find out how effective traditional cures can be. A German tourist murmurs gratefully as hotel staff rub in milk from the cactus leaf to soothe his bright red sunburn.

Fruits

Sri Lanka has a delicious array of fresh fruits. These are popular for breakfast and also as desserts. Some fruits would be quite familiar to someone from Britain (for example, bananas, melons, pineapples, avocadoes . . .). Others are an unusual treat.

The *rambutan* is about the size of a tangerine and covered in soft red spines. ("*Rambutan*" is actually a Malaysian word meaning "spiny".) You peel off the spiny skin to find something like a lychee.

The *mangosteen* is about the size of a small apple. Its skin is dark purple. Inside there are pure white segments (rather like orange segments) with a sweet-sour flavour.

The custard apple is about the size of a grapefruit but shaped more like a pear. Its thin skin is light green. These fruits are ready to eat when they feel somewhat soft.

33 Breadfruit is another very large fruit similar to
jak fruit and which is also cooked in curries. The
photograph shows how breadfruit pieces are left to
dry in the sun before cooking. What fruits do you eat
that are eaten cooked as a vegetable as well?

Mangoes come in a variety of shapes. The green-skinned type produced in the north around Jaffna has a texture much like a peach.

A jak fruit is quite large – about water-melon size. It breaks into hundreds of bright orange/yellow segments. The fruit is often cooked in curries as a vegetable. If cooked when young, with spices, it tastes about like chicken. "Poor man's chicken" is a nickname for the fruit. The government has banned the cutting down of jak trees (which were being used for wood) so that the poor can get the fruits. For poorer families who cannot buy much meat or fish, jak fruit is an important source of protein.

Desserts

Besides fresh fruits, there are several other favourite desserts. Curd made from buffalo meat, with treacle poured over, is popular, as are baked bananas with honey. A variety of desserts are made by mixing rice flour, palm sugar, cinnamon, nutmeg and cardamom. *Pani pol* is a sticky cake made with coconut and honey. *Kiributh* combines rice, coconut and honey. There is of course a coconut cake. *Thalaguli* (sesame ball) is well-liked, as is *bibikan* – a Sinhalese cake made of rice flour, palm sugar, coconut, cashews and dried fruit.

"Hot" and "cold" foods

In much of Asia, food is divided into opposite categories of "hot" and "cold". There is also a group of "in-between" foods. These categories do not refer to the actual

34 Water-buffalo curd (yoghurt) is sold in earthenware bowls in markets and at roadside stalls. It is often eaten at breakfast, and also as a dessert with treacle.

RECIPE
Wattalappan
(popular dessert in Sri Lanka)

1 lb jaggery (palm sugar) (dark brown
  sugar may be used)
1½ cups water
10 eggs
1 pint milk
1 tsp vanilla essence
6 cardamoms
4 cloves
1 tsp cinnamon powder

Mix the cardamoms and cloves together as a powder.
Heat the sugar in 1½ cups of water until it dissolves. Then let it cool.
Beat the egg yolks with the spices. Add the melted sugar and the milk and beat again. Add vanilla.
Beat the egg whites till stiff and add slowly to the milk mixture. Pour the mixture into a greased bowl and steam for 45 minutes.

Do you need a cooker for this recipe or could you make it over an open fire?

35 A typical kitchen in rural Sri Lanka. Most people, in rural areas especially, cook over open fires with wood or coconut husks and other wastes as fuel. Most food is stewed in traditional clay "chutty" pots, but metal pans are being used increasingly as well.

temperature of the foods, nor to their immediate effects on the body. For example, ice-cream is actually in the category of "heaty" food. Nearly all meat and eggs are cooling. Hot foods act to increase heat in the body, while cool foods have the opposite effect. Examples of some "heaty" vegetables are cabbage and tomatoes. Some cooling vegetables are spinach, cucumber and leeks. A balanced diet with both heaty and cooling foods is needed. This is part of the general Asian belief in harmony and balance in life. Sri Lankan cooking tries to combine foods from the different categories in this way.

Food as a gift

Celebrations on the island nearly always involve the sharing of food. "*Dana*" is the word for any kind of gift, but in fact the gift of food is so common that speaking of "*dana*" often refers to the sharing of food. Food is offered to relatives, neighbours, strangers, monks, beggars.

I wandered close to families out picnicking by a stream. Smiling and hoping just to be allowed to take their photo, I was greeted and delicious food was instantly pressed into my hand. Again as I wandered close to a family by a van at a game park, several rich cakes ("homemade") were immediately offered. Sharing food is just part of the warmth and hospitality shown by so many Sri Lankans.

6
The Hill Country and Kandy

The Mahaweli River Project

Sri Lanka's need for energy prompted the massive Mahaweli River Project, begun in 1970. By the mid-1980s the Mahaweli scheme had produced four dams and power stations, plus a canal, and involved work on thousands of hectares of land. The scheme will mean much more irrigated land and also much more hydro-electric power for homes and industry. The Victoria Dam was built largely with funds from British overseas aid. This one dam, which began filling in 1984, will be increasing electricity on the island by about 40%.

The Mahaweli River is in an area in the centre-south of Sri Lanka. This area of higher land is called the Hill Country. Steep hills average over 914 metres (3000 feet) and some peaks are over twice this high. The climate is somewhat cooler than elsewhere on the island. Cascading waterfalls and caves can be seen as you drive along the winding roads. Why is this a good area to develop power using water as a source of energy?

Tea country

The most lasting impression of the Hill Country is tea. The hills are carpeted with tea bushes up and down the valleys. Sri Lanka is the world's third largest grower of tea and the world's largest exporter. Tea needs a warm climate to grow, with rainfall of 178 cm (about 70") or more per year. Since the bushes also grow best at higher altitudes, it is not surprising that the central Hill Country is where most of Sri Lanka's tea is found.

Tea is very much a legacy of the British colonial era. The plants were brought to the island in the mid-nineteenth century. Wide areas of land were cleared and the planters needed labourers to work on their plantations. To fill the need, the planters brought in workers from the Tamil areas of South India. Today it is still descendants of these Indian Tamils who work on the tea estates.

"Little England"

In the heart of tea country is Nuwara Eliya, dubbed "Little England". The area is a curious relic of Victorian colonial times. A British hunting expedition came to the site in 1819 and a health resort was established six years later. The explorer Sir Samuel Baker stayed here in 1846 and returned in 1848 to create an "English village". Baker brought hounds, domestic staff, sheep, cattle, farming tools – even a horse and carriage. The carriage did not survive the mountainous journey, but the rest of the experiment lasted eight years. A legacy today are the Hereford and Durham cows, as well as the types of vegetables (potatoes, leeks . . .) grown.

Most English of all is the Hill Club, a grey stone mansion built in 1876. It has all the atmosphere of a traditional English gentlemen's club. There are overstuffed chairs in the lounge and mounted heads of leopard and bear on the wall. Dinner is served by candlelight by waiters wearing white gloves. Men must wear a tie – and can rent one if caught unprepared.

36 A tea factory in the central Hill Country. Tea leaves are picked by women from bushes all around, and then processed here. Men do most of the factory work. The leaves are first withered at the top level of the factory, to lose moisture. Withered leaves then drop down to a lower floor, where they are rolled to get out the sap. The leaves are next fermented at a high temperature and then dried. Dried leaves must be sorted, sifted and graded into different types and qualities. On the ground floor, loose tea is packed into foil-lined chests for sending overseas. The tea is sold through auctions in Colombo. Only about 10% of Sri Lanka's tea is packeted in the country. (The colonial pattern was to export loose tea, and this continues today.) Sri Lanka would like to packet more of its tea, as this would mean more jobs and earnings for the island.

Most tea estates were nationalized in the 1970s and are now owned by the Sri Lankan government rather than by British companies. However, there are still British (and other foreigners) working in Sri Lanka on a variety of jobs. Many British still congregate at the Hill Club, often coming for long weekends from Colombo. Overheard at the bar was a woman who buys flowers by the yard to decorate her table for dinner parties. She was complaining that those in her own garden were taken by servants and sold at the gate for temple flowers.

37 The Hill Club in Nuwara Eliya, built by the ▶ English in 1876 as a club for Europeans. Does it look as if it might be in England?

38   Maithri C. Samarasinghe is General Manager of an engineering company in Colombo, making prefabricated steel buildings. He is a member of the Royal Colombo Golf Club and occasionally stays at the Hill Club for golf tournaments. The Hill Club was only for Europeans in colonial days, but that has changed. (Television became available on the island only in the late 1970s and was still not widespread by the mid-1980s. There are two channels broadcasting in the evenings.)

Near the Hill Club are houses of a familiar English style. There is also the golf course — one of only two in Sri Lanka — and the racecourse, which has now been closed. (Betting shops in Colombo are very busy — but it is races in *England* that are the subject of bets!)

Nearly next door to the Hill Club is the Grand Hotel, an Elizabethan-style inn. The town even has a "Victoria Park". Fishermen enjoy the trout-filled lake, but this too is England re-created. Trout are not native to Sri Lanka. Twenty-five were brought from England in 1882 to begin stocking the streams.

Adam's Peak

A high point of the Hill Country (in every sense) is Adam's Peak, 2,243 metres (7,360 feet) high. All the main religions of Sri Lanka regard this as a holy mountain. Since the eleventh century, and possibly earlier, the mountain has been

39 *The city of Kandy. Which direction would you follow from Colombo to reach Kandy? Which direction would you follow from Nuwara Eliya to reach Kandy? The lake is artificial and was built in 1807 by the last ruler of the Kingdom of Kandy.*

climbed by pilgrims – tens of thousands every year. Most climb at night by a staircase lit by lamps. There are "rests" and refreshment stalls along the way.

The city of Kandy

Kandy (named from the Sinhalese word "Kanda", meaning "hill") is Sri Lanka's second city. As the city is 488 metres (1600 feet) above sea level, the name is a good one. Kandy is only about 115 km (72 miles) inland from the main city Colombo and is the centre of traditional Sri Lankan arts and culture. While the coastal regions of the island were taken over by European powers, the Kingdom of Kandy was able to resist for 300 years longer. It was not until 1815 that the British managed to control Kandy as well.

The Municipal Market has all the bustle of a traditional market. Stalls sell fruits and fabrics, baskets and buckets. In the centre is a stand for the National Development Lottery. Bets of 1 or 2 rupees are placed. Cash prizes are awarded, and the rest of the money is used to build wells and to support students. About half of Sri Lanka's university students are on scholarships. Many of these are paid for by lottery funds.

The Kandyan Arts and Crafts Association, founded in the early 1880s, sells a wide range of crafts, from silver and brass metalwork to lacquerwork, wood carving, pottery and weaving.

Just outside Kandy are such sights as an "Elephant Orphanage". Young elephants found abandoned or injured in jungle areas are raised to maturity. The animals are trained to work and eventually sold.

The Botanical Gardens

Also just outside Kandy are the Botanical Gardens, established in 1816. The 65 hectares (147 acres) of garden include examples of all Sri Lanka flora, and samples of overseas species as well. There is Agathis Robusta, the chunky Elephant's Leg Tree used for making matchsticks. Giant bamboo is used for making drums, walking sticks and scaffolding. It grows 30 centimetres (one foot) a day (!) and is cut after three years.

There are 10,000 big trees in the garden. The largest is the 120-year-old Java Fig picnic tree which can cover a picnic for 1000 people at once. The Avenue of Royal Palms is lined by 200 trees. Along the Bat Drive "flying dogs" (bats) hang in the trees. Traditional belief is that bad people are re-born as flying dogs. Bats eat fruits, seeds and tender leaves and so are a nuisance to villagers.

There are fifty varieties of palm shown in the garden, including the "Needle Palm". This makes monkeys angry because they cannot climb it. Betel-nut palm provides betel-leaf and nut. Many Sri Lankans habitually chew betel, rather like smoking. Betel is a traditional offering to make amends after an argument.

There are also examples of the 150-year-old rubber trees brought to Sri Lanka by the British. Different kinds of grasses are shown as well. One type is well-suited for crickets, another for rabbits – and yet another for grazing water-buffalo.

Fifteen varieties of temple flowers are shown, including the cannonball flower. Our guide reported that young ladies offer this to Lord Buddha saying that they "want a good husband without drinking arrack". (Arrack is an alcoholic drink made from coconut palm toddy.) Over 500 varieties of orchids are shown in an orchid house.

The Botanical Gardens are bounded on three sides by the Mahaweli River. As we look across, a woman is washing herself by the water – a sight familiar at standpipes and rivers all over this lush, lovely island.

◄ 40   *Cinema poster, Kandy. Film-going is very popular in Sri Lanka. The lettering on the sign is in Sinhala. Does it look similar to any other writing you have seen? What words on the poster would make a person from the UK feel very much at home?*

7
Minority people

The Tamils

The Hill Country is home for many of Sri Lanka's largest minority group, the Tamils, who make up 20% of the island's population. Tea and Tamils are linked in Sri Lanka, as it was Tamils from South India who were brought to work the tea estates. ("Tamil" is the name for people living in the southern Indian state of Tamil Nadu.) When coffee was the island's main plantation crop, in the mid-nineteenth century, immigrants came from South India to help with the harvests. They returned home

41 Tamil women picking tea. They move amongst the bushes, plucking the new top leaves only. These can be plucked every five or six days. The women carry baskets on their backs to hold the leaves they collect.

Tea bushes grow best on higher land. Why is most of the island's tea grown in the south-central area?

The Land Reform Act of 1972 began a "nationalization" of the plantations. By 1975, all the tea estates were owned by the Sri Lankan government.

42   Two waiters. Lal Ratnayake (left) is Sinhalese.
S.J. Chandrakumar ("Chandra") (right) is a Tamil.
Chandra's parents are from South India and had a
shop in Kandy. This was burned in 1983 at a time of
serious violence between the Sinhalese and Tamils.
His parents then went back to South India.
   In the background is Sigiriya Rock, the huge stone
which held a palace in the sky in the fifth century.
See page 16.

after the coffee beans were picked. When tea and rubber began to replace coffee, labour was needed all year round. Tamils were brought as a permanent cheap workforce. Tamil tea workers are still among the poorest people in the country today.

However, two-thirds of the Tamils in Sri Lanka are part of a much older community that has lived in Sri Lanka for many centuries. They are proud to be descended from South Indian invaders of the island in the second and third centuries A.D. Over 90% of the people in the northern province are these *Jaffna* Tamils (Jaffna being the main city in the far north). The eastern coast has many of these people, too, called "Jaffna Tamils" even when they have moved elsewhere on the island. (Jaffna is the driest part of the island, and fairly flat. Farmers there need deep wells to help irrigate the land. Onions, chillies, rice, tobacco and other vegetables are the main crops.)

Jaffna Tamils are in fact employed in many professions. As well as farmers, there are doctors, engineers, accountants, managers. Tamils feel it is partly their success in academic and other professions which has prompted jealousy from the Sinhalese majority.

There has been conflict between the Sinhalese and Tamils for many centuries. In 237 B.C. Tamils invaded from South India and ruled the northern part of the island for 22 years. This happened again, as when the Pandyans invaded from South India in the ninth century A.D. The Sinhalese people have heard the stories of the past and have come to feel that the Tamils are the historical enemy of the nation. For example, Tamils have been blamed for the collapse of the island's irrigation civilization in the thirteenth century. Anti-Tamil feeling in the country has led many Tamils to want a separate area for themselves. (Tamils on the tea estates are somewhat apart from Jaffna Tamils, but they too have faced problems.)

In recent years, Jaffna Tamils have demanded a separate Tamil state, called "Elem", in the north (which is virtually a Tamil homeland already). Changes in the Constitution in the 1970s made Tamils feel they had less part than before in running the country. The Tamil Tigers are a group that has used violence and bombings to further its cause. For the Sinhalese majority (70% of the island's population), who have wanted no separate Tamil state, actions by the Tamil Tigers have been seen as "terrorist activity". For minority Tamils, the "terrorists" have been seen as "freedom fighters". Over 5000 people (both Tamil and Sinhalese) died in the struggles between 1983 and 1987. The conflict might be another reason for calling the island the "teardrop" of India.

Can you think of other places in the world where there is conflict between different cultural groups, with different religions, living in the same country?

Tamils dress much the same as the Sinhalese, often wearing European-style dress in urban areas especially. However, there are slight differences. Tamil men traditionally wear the *verti*, a long length of cotton from waist to ankles, with a long-sleeved shirt. Jaffna Tamil women wrap their sari in a slightly different way from Sinhalese women.

An important Tamil custom is the tying of the *thali* at a wedding. This is a gold necklace with an inscribed medallion. Another custom which is still followed in rural areas happens when a Tamil girl comes of age. She is kept apart from everyone for about 16 days, in a hut made of freshly cut coconut palm leaves. After this time she has a ritual bath and is fed a diet of raw eggs, sesame oil and *pittu*, made from millet or rice flour. (There is a ceremony like this for Sinhalese girls as well, with spice soup.)

One effect of change on the island for all groups is that some traditions are no longer followed as strictly as before. The influence of Western ideas, growing cities and industries is that some restrictions are fading. For example, Tamil tradition says that a widow may no longer wear gold jewellery or bright saris. This tradition is not often followed on the island today.

43　A Hindu temple on the south coast. The temple
is organized to be like a human body. The entrance,
with its carved and colourful figures, is symbolic of
the feet. Main images are in the temple's "head".
Offerings are made in what is the temple's
"stomach". Can you see any animals in the
carvings?

Burghers

The word "Burgher" is Dutch for "town-dweller". It is the term used on the island to describe those descended from Dutch colonists. It is also used more generally for any Sri Lankan descended from European colonists – including the Portuguese and British. Burghers generally live in towns and cities, and wear European-style clothes. They are Christian in faith.

Veddhas

Several thousand Veddhas (primitive tribal people) live on the island. Many have now left their traditional hunting and gathering in the jungle and have become settled farmers. Racially, these Veddhas are somewhat like the Australian aborigines and the African Bushmen. ("*Veddha*" is the Sinhalese word for "hunter".)

Hinduism

About 80% of Sri Lankan Tamils follow the Hindu religion. (Most of the other Tamils are Christian, mainly Roman Catholics.) There is no single set of beliefs that all Hindus follow, but most in Sri Lanka are "Shaivites" (regarding the god Shiva as supreme).

Hinduism has a variety of gods and goddesses. The deity Aiyamar (who protects agriculture) is one especially worshipped by farmers in the dry Tamil areas. *Puja* involves ritual offerings to gods. Hindus generally believe that life is made of five elements, earth, water, fire, wind and *akasha* (ether), and the offerings they make symbolize each of these elements. The offerings are presented at dawn and dusk *puja* hours at Hindu temples. Drums beat, bugles are blown, bells are rung. *Devala* is the word for a larger shrine, while *kovril* is a smaller temple.

Gypsies

Groups of gypsies wander across the island and set up camps on unoccupied land. They travel in bands of about 15-25 people (several families), using donkeys to carry their belongings. One group of gypsies, the *Ahikuntakaya*, are known for their ability to train cobras to dance to the tunes of flutes. (The snakes are really reacting to movements of the gypsy's body and flute – not to the sound.) Other gypsies are monkey-trainers, and others specialize in tattooing. Gypsy women often make beads, hats or baskets, or tell fortunes by reading palms. Gypsies are somewhat apart from Sri Lankan society and have their own annual gathering in November in the North Central Province.

*44 A gypsy entertains with snake-charming. ▶
It is the movement of the hands and pipe rather than the sound which causes the snakes to rise. The snakes are deadly cobras, but their venom has been taken away.*

At temples there is also the chanting of *vedas*. These are a collection of over 1,000 hymns written in about 1700 B.C. by the first Aryan invaders in North India.

Sri Lanka's Jaffna Tamils keep a rigid division of castes. Brahmans are the highest and purest caste of people. Next comes the *vellala*, or farming caste. Below this are craftsmen. Lower still are such workers as fishermen and barbers. The lowest castes cannot sit at the same level or eat with higher-caste Tamils.

Hindus believe in the idea of reincarnation (life after death). Each person accepts his or her station in life, knowing that it is payment for what he or she did in the previous life. How you behave in this life will help your role in the next life.

A visible sign of Hindu devotion is the *tikka*, the "divine eye". This is a mixture of sandalwood paste or holy ash put on the forehead above and between the eyes.

Muslims

About 7% of Sri Lanka's population is Muslim. These people are found throughout the country, but live especially along the south-west and east coasts and in towns and cities.

There are actually two groups of Sri Lankan Muslims. Most are descended from the Arab traders who settled in Sri Lanka from the eighth century A.D. They are known as the "Moors". The other Muslims are from Malaysia. Muslims around Hambantota are mainly Malay. For both groups, Arabic is the language for religious teaching and prayer, but Tamil is used in schools.

The voice of the *muezzin* calls the devout Muslim to prayer five times a day. Men and women are kept separate for worship. Women are generally somewhat restricted to the home. They must cover their heads and lower faces when out on the street. Muslims do not eat pork, and their food is generally sweeter than Sinhalese or Tamil cooking.

8

Ride around the south coast

Many of the island's Muslims live in Galle, a town on the south-west coast with a good natural harbour. This was the island's first major port and Arabs made it a centre for the ivory and gem trade. Sri Lanka's Portuguese and Dutch past is seen there as well, especially near the seventeenth-century Dutch fort. The town of Galle is just one of the sights on a fascinating ride around the south coast to Colombo. As you follow the ride, think about how the coast is a valuable source of economic activity.

Matara City is also a former Arab trading port. An unusual sight there are carriages with red upholstery. These "taxis" are drawn by bullocks through the narrow streets, as they have been for hundreds of years.

Between Matara and Tangalla, at a place called Mawella, there is a blowhole. There are only half a dozen of these known in the world and this is the second largest. Water is trapped in a fissure in a sea-level cave, then forced up by pressure of waves. The water spouts as high as 18 metres (60 feet), straight up through a hole in the rocks.

Further round the coast at Weligama is another unusual sight. In the water are fishermen perched on long poles, each pole with a small platform seat. These are the famous "stilt" fishermen of Weligama. Each pole is family-owned and passed on from father to son. There is fishing from boats at Weligama as well. The catch is brought in and sorted by

45 A "stilt" fisherman at Weligama. What are the advantages and disadvantages of fishing this way?

the shore. Bicycles with large boxes carry the fish to markets in town.

If you are lucky, you may be driving around the coast just as a seine is being hauled in. The seine is a large net, 1 to 1.5 km long. One end is taken out to sea by fishermen in a big canoe. The fishermen first watch to see where birds are catching fish or where fish are seen jumping in the water. The other end of the net is held on the beach. When the sea end of the net is brought in, the fish are trapped. The seine hangs like a curtain in the water, with wooden floats at the top edge and sinkers (stones) at the bottom.

It may take hours to haul in the long net, with much of the village helping. The men chant and sing as they stand in lines and heave in the net. Children rush about excitedly, helping to spread the net on the shore. Everyone who helps takes some part of what is caught. The net must then be spread out, repaired and made ready for the next time. No shore-seining takes place during the monsoons, as the water is too rough.

Diving

The water around Sri Lanka's south coast is an attraction for undersea divers as well as fishermen. The Indian Ocean has coral reefs,

46 A seine (large net) is being hauled in. Everyone who helps takes some share of the fish that are caught. Why are there pieces of wood attached to the net?

fish life and offshore shipwrecks to view. The clarity of the water changes with the monsoon seasons and other conditions, so diving is best in certain months. Near Ambalangoda, on the south-west coast, there is very good rock- and reef-diving. Hikkaduwa is another popular centre. (It is sometimes called "Hippieduwa" because of all the young foreigners who gather there, living cheaply, enjoying the sun and sea.)

Colombo

The ride round the south coast leads to Colombo, which is now Sri Lanka's largest city and business centre. There has been some settlement there since the eighth century A.D. Arab traders used it as a port for shipping cinnamon. When the Portuguese came in the early sixteenth century, other things were shipped as well, such as sapphire gems. The Dutch followed in the seventeenth century and built a fort. The commercial section is still called "Fort" from those early times.

The fort has brown stone buildings which were the National State Assembly, the

44

47   A street scene in the pettah area of Colombo.
Now the island's main city, Colombo was not one of
the most ancient cities. Why would overseas
colonial rulers (the Portuguese, the Dutch, the
British) want a city on the coast with a good port?   48   Central Colombo.

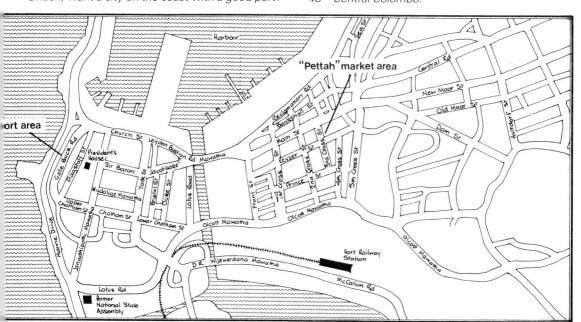

parliament. Since the early 1980s the government buildings have been moved to an island in a small lake, just seven miles (11 km) east of Colombo. At Sri Jayawardhanapura Kotte there are new parliament buildings and government offices.

The President's house is still in Colombo's fort area. Sri Lanka is a democratic republic with a President, Prime Minister and M.P.s. Since a new constitution was approved in 1978, the government has adopted some of the features of the American and French systems. The President has now become head of state. Another big change is that voters now vote for a party, not an individual candidate.

One area of Colombo, full of street sellers, is called the *pettah* – bazaar district. The word "*pettah*" comes from a Tamil word meaning "outside". Look at figure 48 showing part of the city. Where was the *pettah* area, in relation to the fort area?

In figure 47 you can see the sign "Sea Street" and a sign for silver traders. Sea Street is mainly for silver and goldsmiths. Other streets are specialized as well. First Cross Street has mainly electrical and photographic goods. Second Cross Street has mainly jewellers, and textiles are sold on Main Street. Tea, spices and traditional herb medicines are sold on Fifth Cross Street. Find the places on the map which you would go to if you wanted to buy a camera, a watch, cinnamon.

Some street names in Colombo are a reminder of the country's past. "Old Moor Street" and "New Moor Street" refer to the early Arab traders who came to the island. The "Cinnamon Gardens" district was once covered with spice plantations. This is now a fashionable housing area, with little cinnamon in sight. What would the street called "York Street" tell you about Sri Lanka's colonial past?

9

Young people

"School pen . . . bonbon . . . you give me . . .".
The tourist car stops in Sri Lanka and children
are drawn to it, as to a magnet, asking for things
or just staring in fascination. They are great fun,
with big smiles – and part of the island's charm.
Some children are selling to tourists – peacock
feathers, unusual rocks or shells. . . . Young
people in Sri Lanka do harder work as well.
They are on the roads, carrying buckets or pots
of water filled from a standpipe or well. They
are minding water-buffalo, helping to paint
masks, or making other craft items.

*49 A boy works at a small sugar-processing plant.
The juice squeezed from sugar-cane is boiled to
make a brown sugar called "jaggery". How old do
you think this boy is? Is the work dangerous for a
young person?*

*50 Sri Lanka is one of over 70 countries in the
world growing sugar-cane. Sugar may be produced
from either sugar-cane or sugar-beet. Cane is grown
in tropical countries while beet is grown in
temperate climates.*
*Which is grown in the UK – cane or beet? Does
cane or beet supply a larger part of the world's
sugar?*

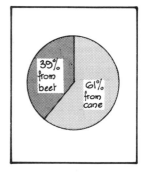

39% from beet
61% from cane

Laws in Sri Lanka set the minimum age for employment at 14. As in other poorer countries, where even small earnings of the children help a family to survive, this law is not always followed. In a survey in the late 1970s, the Anti-Slavery Society found that half the children in their research were in employment at an earlier age than 14. On the tea estates in Sri Lanka, children from the age of five may be potting seedlings. From the age of 12, young people may be working on other jobs, such as weeding. There are schools on the estates, but these are poorly equipped. Children of tea estate workers have less chance for education – and they are about twice as likely as other children in Sri Lanka to die as babies. About 85% of tea estate children are malnourished (without the foods they need for good health).

To someone coming to Sri Lanka from a richer country in Europe or North America, many children, and not just those on tea estates, seem small for their age. Overall, about a quarter of children on the island are undernourished. They do not get enough of the foods they need for good health. It is a surprise to ask the age of a boy who looks about 10 – and be told he is 15. A girl who looks about eight may really be age 12. This is true for many poorer countries in the world.

Population control

Young people have a better chance of being properly fed, clothed, housed and educated if they are not part of a rapidly growing population. Such a population puts pressure on resources: there is simply less to go round.

The population of a country depends on both its *birth rate* and its *death rate*. The *birth rate* is the number of live births in a given year for each 1000 of the population. The *death rate* is the number of people dying in a given year, for each 1000 of the population. In the world today, more babies are surviving. More and more people are living to an older age. As more babies survive and more people live longer, the *death* rate goes down. Better medical care and better living conditions have been helping to lower death rates. Unless people also have fewer children and so lower the *birth* rate, the population grows quickly.

In Europe and North America, populations began to grow more slowly in the nineteenth century. In much of Asia, Africa and Latin America, until the mid-1960s, the rate of growth was rising. Population was growing especially fast in these areas after the Second World War. Medical care and improved living conditions began to result in markedly lower death rates. Meanwhile, the size of families was still large.

Over the last few decades, many countries have started to encourage smaller families. The first country in the world to have this policy was India, in 1952. Since the mid-1960s, birth rates have been falling nearly everywhere, except in Africa south of the Sahara.

Sri Lanka is an example of a country where the birth rate has been falling since the 1960s. But if you look at the table below, you will see that families in Sri Lanka are still larger, on average, than families in the richer UK:

Annual population growth rate (%):	Average number of children per woman:
UK −0.1	1.7
Sri Lanka 2.1	3.6
(1984 figures)	

There are valid reasons why people in most of the world's poorer countries still choose to have more children, on average, than people in richer countries. Although the number of children who die has fallen sharply, it is still higher in poorer countries than in wealthier ones. In poorer countries, parents still feel the need to have more babies, to be sure that at least some of their children will survive. In most poorer countries it is still children who look after their parents when they are old. Children in poorer countries are also useful to their parents – helping with farming, family industries and sometimes working for wages as well. Children help with the chores of daily

51　*There are ten children in this fisherman's family living near the south coast. This is larger than the usual family size. Most families are now having fewer children than families years ago. Family planning programmes have been very successful in slowing the rate of population growth.*

Note that two of the boys are wearing a sarama, *the traditional tied cloth covering for a male.*

Compare this house to the thatched-roof home on page 9. How is it different? How can you tell that this family is not among the poorest on the island?

Look at figure 52 (page 50). Is the part of the population under age 15 greater in Sri Lanka or in the UK? Is the part of the population over age 64 greater in Sri Lanka or in the UK? How is a country affected if it has a larger part of the people as young? How is a country affected if it has a larger part of the people as old?

	INDIA	SRI LANKA	UK
average life expectancy at birth (1982)	55 yrs	69 yrs	74 yrs
infant mortality rate (deaths per 1000 live births, 1981)	94	32	12

life, such as carrying water and firewood. By contrast, children in richer countries today are more of a cost to their parents — and do not contribute as much work.

As people become richer and have better living conditions, they tend to *want* smaller families. Also, as women have better chances for education and jobs, they tend to want fewer children. Making methods of birth control more available is only part of helping to encourage smaller families. Sri Lanka has a very successful family planning programme, with increasing numbers of couples using contraceptives to control family size.

In which country do young people have the best chance to live to an old age? In which country do babies have the least chance of surviving? Using figure 52 and the table above, what general points could you make about Sri Lanka in relation to India? in relation to the UK?

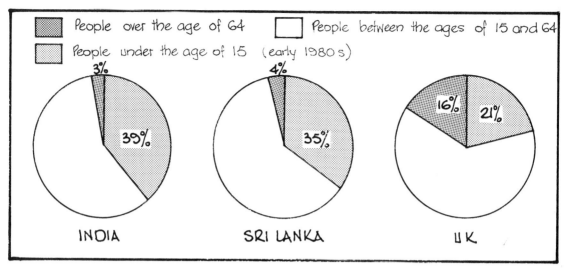

People over the age of 64   People between the ages of 15 and 64

People under the age of 15   (early 1980s)

3%
39%
INDIA

4%
35%
SRI LANKA

16% 21%
UK

52   The proportions of different age-groups in Sri Lanka, India and the UK.

53   A rural health centre. Since the 1970s, Sri Lanka has developed a wide network of free health services. The level of health is impressively high for a country so poor.

Schools

Sri Lanka is a poor island, but a high proportion of the people (85%) can read and write. (In other countries as poor, only about 40% of the people are literate.) Free education became widespread in the 1970s.

Nearly all the island's children start school at age five. By secondary level, only about 51% are still attending. This sounds low compared to the 83% enrolment at UK secondary schools – but 51% is very high for a country as poor as Sri Lanka. In rural areas especially, children often drop out to help with farming, minding animals and the many chores and small industries that keep life going.

54 A village school. The small shrine at the left is Buddhist, used for morning assembly prayers. There are blackboards and books but almost no other teaching aids. Why are the sides of the classroom left open, with no doors or windows?

Years ago, *all* lessons were taught in English. Sinhalese is now used and children learn English as a separate subject, in just one or two periods a day. No other foreign language is taught until university level. History, Geography and Civics are combined as a single subject called "Social Education".

Children from age five right up to age 17 are usually in one school together. Most schools start at about 7:30 in the morning and end at 1:00 or 1:30. During a break of about 15 minutes, young people can buy sweets and drinks at a small school shop. Most schools have cement wells to supply water. Younger children may bring their safe water (already boiled) from home in a thermos flask.

Schools are usually mixed, and forty children to a class is common. Although the government supplies free textbooks, young people must buy their own plastic biros. Tourists to Sri Lanka face an amusing barrage from local children asking for "school pens".

55 Village pupils walking home from school at 1-1.30 p.m. Many of the girls wear plaited hair and spotless white uniforms. There is no running water in their homes – and no automatic washing machines!

◄ 56 Girl science students at a university near Kandy. About half of the island's students are on scholarships.

Sports

Volleyball is a favourite game amongst young people on the island. It is also common to see groups of boys playing cricket. Cricket and rugby are the most popular sports in Sri Lanka, both drawing large crowds. The season for cricket is September to April, and in 1982 Sri Lanka became a full member of the International Cricket Conference. The rugby season is April to August. Why do you think it is at that time of the year?

Sri Lankans also enjoy tennis and table tennis. Football (soccer) is played locally, but Sri Lanka has no team playing internationally. Badminton and squash have also become popular in recent years. For adults, a less common sport is golf. There are only two clubs on the island, both begun by the British.

Games and toys

Most young people do not have all the commercial toys and games you see in a country like Britain. If you see boys on the island playing draughts, they may well be using bottle-tops for the pieces. Children in villages like walking on stilts, which are rough home-made poles of local wood.

One toy seen lined up for sale outside furniture shops is a small wooden rocking-horse seat with horse-head. The few "toys" that are available are generally sold with other household goods. A general store in Nuwara Eliya included a few toy machine-guns and dolls made in Hong Kong.

57 A typical bedroom in a thatched village house. ▶ The kerosene lamps are lit at night, as there is no electricity. (An increasing number of homes do have bare electric bulb lights.) What can you see under the girl's bed?

10

Traditional celebrations, dance and crafts

Festivals

Young people also enjoy festival days and celebrations. These are a way of keeping a link with the past and traditions, while much on the island is changing. Ceremonies are held in Sri Lanka for all sorts of occasions — from harvesting rice to laying foundations for a building. The most elaborate ceremonies are those connected to religious occasions.

The Kandy Perahera

From its small beginnings in the fourth century A.D., the Kandy *Perahera* has now become one of the most spectacular pageants in the world. It was King Magavanna (ruling 301-331 A.D.) who said that the Buddha's tooth relic (see page 14) should be paraded for homage once a year. A *perahera* (procession) was begun.

In today's *perahera*, a copy of the tooth relic, contained in a dagoba-shaped casket, is carried on the back of a huge elephant adorned with colourful cloth. The procession includes many other attractions, such as dancers of various kinds and acrobats. On the seventh night, the Kandy *Perahera* is at its best — and 100 or more elephants may be seen.

Nearly all Buddhist temples on the island have their own *peraheras* once a year. Everyone in the village contributes. There are small processions of schoolchildren, drummers and dancers.

Wesak

The full moon day of May and the day following are *Wesak*. These days are the most holy in the Buddhist calendar. *Wesak* celebrates the birth, enlightenment and death of the Buddha.

All major towns celebrate at *Wesak*. The festivities are especially colourful in Colombo. Large *pandals* (bamboo frameworks) are put up along the streets and hung with paintings about the Buddha's life. Lights are everywhere. Coconut-oil lamps (*pol-thel pahana*) line the driveways and courtyards of temples. Pantomimes tell Buddhist tales. Little sheds called *damselas* are put up by roadsides. People give out rice and curry and sweetmeats.

Poson

The full moon day in June is *Poson*, next in importance after *Wesak* for Buddhists. *Poson* marks the coming of Buddhism to the island over 2000 years ago, when a king of Anuradhapura was converted. *Poson* is celebrated throughout Sri Lanka, but is most important in Anuradhapura and Mihintale. Temples are crowded, streets are lit up and decorated.

Kataragama Festival

In July/August there is a two-week festival at Kataragama. This is a place of worship for Hindus, Buddhists, Muslims and some Christians as well. Most who take part in the festival are Hindus.

Self-mortification, believed to be in repayment of vows to the gods, is a feature of these celebrations. Some people put small spears through their cheeks, or roll in hot scorching sand. Fire-walking (walking over hot

58 *Fire-walking (walking over hot burning embers) is part of some celebrations. Here tourists watch with amazement as a dancer performs.*

burning embers) is also done. Colourful flags and lights decorate. There is a blowing of conch shells and a beating of drums. A grand *perahera* comes at the end of the festival.

Vel Procession

Each year in August, a great gilded temple cart (*vel*) is pulled by hundreds of Hindu worshippers from a temple in Colombo to a *kovil* (Hindu temple) several miles to the south. This is supposed to be the *vel* of Skanda, the god of war. The procession takes about a day, with stops for ceremonies. The return journey by night is faster and very colourful. Hundreds of electric bulbs line the route.

Other Hindu festivals

There are a number of other Hindu celebrations. An interesting one in January is called *Madu Pongal*. Each home's domestic animals – from cows and draught-oxen to goats and dogs – are washed and specially fed. The animals have a smear of red marked on the forehead, and they are garlanded with flowers.

In late October is *Deepavali*, the Festival of Lights. Hindu homes are decorated, new clothes are worn, and lamps are lit to welcome Lakshmi, the goddess of wealth.

Muslim festivals

Most Muslim festivals are celebrated by holding public meetings for group prayers, and at home with prayer and reading of the Koran (holy book). For *Id-ul-Fitr* there are great feasts to end the fasting of the previous four weeks of *Ramazan*.

The New Year

April is the time of the new year for both the Sinhalese and the Tamils. On the eve of the new year, it is traditional to clean homes and light small lamps. People then spend some time in religious celebrations. When the new year comes in, a fire is lit in the kitchen, new clothes are put on, and new activities are started. The *gana-denu* ("give-and-take") begins. Sri Lankans exchange money with someone close to them. New year ceremonies end with an anointing ceremony. Oil is mixed with herbal paste. A family elder rubs a spot of this on the head of each person in the family.

The new year is also a time for games and sports.

Dance

Sri Lankan dance is dazzling in movement and colour. Costumes are lavish. Drummers add to the frenzy and spectacle on stage. There are some similarities to Indian classical dance, but Sri Lankan dance relies much more on vigorous body movement, footwork and even acrobatics.

There are two distinct types of dance on the island. "Low-country dancing" is a form of devil-dancing performed most in the south. It uses theatrics such as mime and impersonation, and often humorous masks. (The purpose of devil-dancing was originally to "drive out" demons from sick people.) "Up-country dancing" is seen more in the north-central area, around the town of Kandy. Up-country Kandy dance is more lyrical than low country dance and is performed by females as well as males.

Dance is an entertainment, but some has a more serious purpose as well. *Sokari* is a folk dance to encourage a good rice crop. In villages of the south there are still ceremonies which include devil-dancing to control evil spirits. If a person is ill and doctors cannot help, such a ceremony may take place at night, including drums, frenzied masked dancing, and a sacrifice – often using the blood of a cock.

Crafts : – Wooden

The *kolam* masks used in dance-drama and masks for devil-dancing are made by craftspeople on the island. Ambalangoda, a town in the south, is a centre for mask-makers. Tourist souvenir masks are carved as well. A soft *kaduru* wood is used.

Other types of carving made in Sri Lanka use mahogany, ebony, coconut wood, teak and other woods. Figures of elephants, Buddhas, tigers, dancing figures, etc, are cut, sanded, waxed and polished.

Some wooden crafts are decorated by a

59   A comic mask is used to entertain in dance-drama.

60   The "18 disease" mask. A demon holding victims in his hands and teeth is surrounded by faces of different diseases. Cobra snakes are shown as well. Such masks are used in devil-dancing to exorcise and drive away ill-health.

The island now has modern health services, but traditional ideas about disease are followed in some village areas. Plant medicines are used widely, as well as modern drugs.

coloured *lac*. This is made of resin from trees, to which colour pigment is added. Lacquer-work boxes are especially attractive.

Baskets

Just as Ambalangoda is famous for masks, so Kalutara, also in the south, is famous for baskets. Woven mats and baskets are practical as well as decorative. Split bamboo or cane (rattan) is used, as well as palm leaves. Everything from grain to chickens may be carried in baskets, so these must be strong and well-made.

Pottery

Potters also produce objects for practical use. Besides lamps for places of worship, water jugs and cooking vessels are needed. The pottery may be decorated by drawing patterns on the wet clay or by stamping in a pattern with a wooden die. Sometimes pots are glazed before firing in a kiln.

Metalwork

Gold and silver rings, earrings, bracelets and chains are "insurance" for Sri Lankans as well as decoration. They are bought when times are good and can be sold to raise funds when times are hard. Silver is also made into spoons, tea-sets and items of that kind.

Other metals are used as well. Brass is made into a variety of pots, plaques and boxes. One method for decorating brass is called "cutwork", when a "cut-out" lacy effect is used. Another technique is called "*repoussé*". This involves hammering the pattern from the reverse side. Sometimes thin sheets of copper or silver are worked into designs on brass.

Batik

A very widespread craft on the island is batik. This Javanese term means literally "wax painting". (Java is an island in Indonesia.) The craft was brought from Indonesia to Sri Lanka and workshops are now everywhere. Besides decorating clothing, batik is used on many objects from lampshades to wall-hangings.

The pattern on the cloth is built up by a series of waxings and dyeings. The design is drawn on to the cloth, and wax is then put on to those areas of the design that are *not* to be dyed. The wax is put on both sides of the cloth. The fabric is placed in a colour of dye and afterwards in boiling water to remove the wax. These steps

are followed for each colour that is used.

Traditional methods are still used for these crafts, but, as with other aspects of life on the island, there are changes. For example, batiks are still hand-produced, but a series of different hands take the cloth through the various stages. An "assembly line" has become common. It used to be that one artist would do all the steps on one batik. (Some artists do still prefer this.)

As with brasswork, woodwork and other crafts, many batiks are shipped for sale overseas or sold locally to tourists. Sri Lankans also hang batik pictures on walls of their homes, and use them to decorate hotels. Pictures may show Kandy dancers, fishermen or other scenes of island life.

61   Examples of Sri Lankan brass-work. Highly-skilled craftspeople produce a wide variety of decorated products. What animals are shown on the items above? Why is the plaque in the bottom right corner a good reminder of a tropical island?

62   Girls paint wax on to fabric to make batik clothes and wall-hangings. Why is wax put on the fabric before it is dipped in a colour dye?

11

Tourism – mixed blessing

Help to the island?

Craft industries sell many of their products to foreign visitors, who have been coming to Sri Lanka in increasing numbers. The warm climate, beautiful beaches, ancient sites, game parks and other places of interest are the attractions. In the late 1960s, the government began a plan to encourage more tourism. While there were only 24,000 visitors in 1967, there were over 400,000 in 1982.

For Sri Lanka, as well as for other places, this tourism is a mixed blessing. More visitors can mean more jobs, but much of the work is seasonal and unreliable. Sri Lankans working in hotels or as drivers or guides may be busy for only part of the year. In the mid-1980s, tourism slumped badly as the Tamil-Sinhalese conflict

(see page 39) led to fighting, burning of shops and even bombs exploding. "Trouble" is not something visitors want on their holiday in the sun!

Tourism is a mixed blessing for other reasons as well. Foreign visitors usually want luxuries. Providing these luxuries can be at the expense of basic improvements for local people. While foreigners at luxury hotels adjust

63   The luxury Hotel Triton on the south-west coast, designed by a Sri Lankan and using many local products. The boat as decoration in the pool is a traditional Sri Lankan fishing craft. About a third of the employees live in the nearby village of Ahungalla. What mixed feelings might these employees have about foreigners who are clearly so much richer than themselves?

their air-conditioning to low, medium or high, Sri Lankans nearby may be without even electricity in their homes.

Using local products

A country's earnings from tourism may be reduced if much is spent on food and goods from abroad to please the visitors. Sri Lankan hotels make good use of local products. This saves money for the country and creates a more interesting experience for the tourist as well.

An example is the Hotel Triton on the south-west coast. Coir matting is used on the floors. Batik pictures decorate the walls. The furniture was all designed and made in Sri Lanka. Even the beach umbrellas are locally produced. Guests returning to their rooms in the evening find white lotus flowers placed on the turned-down sheets.

Sigiriya Village is a hotel also designed to reflect Sri Lankan culture. In the Temple Wing, the rooms use colours as seen in Buddhist temples. (These are usually white, contrasting starkly with the yellow robes of priests and the wood shades of carvings.) Copper and earthenware are commonly seen in temples. These materials are used for lampshades and waste-paper baskets in the hotel rooms. Appliquéd and hand-woven collages show scenes associated with temple life. The gardens outside the rooms are typical of a temple courtyard.

64 A mosquito net in a "rest house" hotel. This is untied and spread at night to cover the person in bed. In the mid-1960s, the disease malaria seemed under control but it has become a problem again. Anopheles mosquitoes have developed resistance to insecticides. By the mid-1980s, over 60 countries (including Sri Lanka) faced growing numbers of malaria cases.

Foods are imported for tourists, but local foods are featured as well. This includes "Sri Lanka Night" buffet dinners at hotels. Tourists enjoying a breakfast of fresh tropical fruits often miss this greatly when the holiday ends.

No place is paradise

The "Splendid Island" has its drawbacks – for no place on earth can be paradise. The fascinating wildlife can itself be a problem. Hundreds of people die each year from rabies and snake bites. One reminder to tourists is the mosquito coil in the hotel bedroom. This is to help keep away the insects which spread the disease malaria. Malaria is still a problem on the island, and visitors take tablets to avoid the fever, which can cause death. At some "rest houses" (inexpensive hotels), there may be mosquito nets over the beds. These are unknotted and spread to completely cover people as they sleep.

Sri Lanka is changing but, despite the changes and problems, a visitor may well agree with what the adventurer Marco Polo said centuries ago:

> "On leaving the Island of Andoman and
> Sailing a thousand miles, a little south of west
> The traveller reaches Ceylon, which is
>   undoubtedly
> The finest Island of its size in all the world."

Further reading

Nance Fyson, *People at Work in Sri Lanka* (Batsford, 1987)
Sri Lanka, Insight Guide (Apa Productions, 1983)
Tony Wheeler, *Sri Lanka, a travel survival kit* (Lonely Planet, 1984)
Sri Lanka (Berlitz Travel Guide, 1981)

Answer to question on page 6.

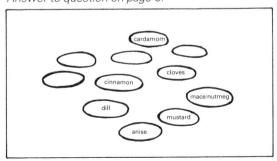

Glossary

arrack fermented alcoholic drink from coconut sap
batik wax painting
bibikan cake of rice flour, palm sugar, coconut, cashews, fried fruit
bithara hoppers with egg in centre
brinjal long egg-plant
Burgher term used for any Sri Lankans descended from European colonists
chena slash-and-burn agriculture
coir fibre from inside coconut shell
copra dried kernel of the coconut
dagoba Buddhist religious monument
dana any gift, especially food
devala larger Hindu shrine
Free Trade Zone area where goods are produced for export; there are tax and other advantages for foreign companies
gokkola knotted coconut palm fronds
gross national product (GNP) total value of goods and services produced within a country, together with payments received from other countries, less similar payments made to other countries
hoppers thin, cup-shaped pancakes
illam coarse, water-borne gravel which contains gems
indiappa "stringhoppers", strings of rice flour dough
jaggery brown sugar
kaduru soft wood used for carving masks
kiribath rice cooked in coconut milk
kovril smaller Hindu temple
lac resin from trees; colour is added and used to decorate crafts
lamprai curried snack
latex milky substance inside rubber trees
maha main rice crop
mahout elephant master

mangosteen small apple, dark purple in colour
monsoons high winds bringing heavy rains at certain times of the year
moonstone semi-circular decorated granite on ground in front of temple
Moors Muslims descended from Arab traders
paddy unhusked rice
pandals bamboo frameworks put up for Wesak celebrations
pansalas Buddhist temples
pettah bazaar district of Colombo
pittu steamed tubes of rice flour, coconut and water
poya days Buddhist holy days linked to phases of the moon
pujas times of religious offerings at Buddhist temples
rambutan tangerine-sized fruit, covered in soft red spines
repoussé a style of decorating brass by hammering the pattern into the metal
roti flatbread made from rice flour, coconut, water
sambol mixture of grated coconut, pickles, onions, lemon juice and sometimes dried fish
samsara re-birth, in Buddhist religion
seine large net used for fishing
thalaguli sesame ball, for dessert
tikka mix of sandalwood paste or holy ash put on forehead above and between eyes on Hindu women
Veddhas primitive tribal people
vel gilded temple cart
vellala farming caste of Hindus
verti Tamil male attire; long length of cotton from waist to ankles
wewas reservoirs in dry zones
yala supplementary rice crop

Island Information

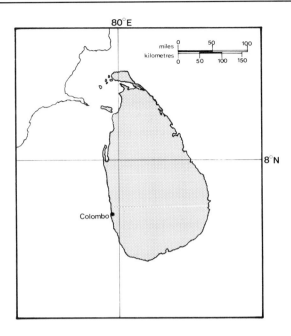

Area: 65,610 sq. km. (25,332 square miles)

Time difference: London   Colombo
                        6.30 a.m.   noon

Currency: monetary unit of Sri Lanka is the rupee (Re or Rs) divided into 100 cents
coins: 1, 2, 5, 10, 25 and 50 cents and Re 1
banknotes: 2, 5, 10, 20, 50 and 100 rupees

Languages (main): 70% Sinhala, 20% Tamil, and English spoken widely

Religions (main): 70% Buddhism, 20% Hinduism, rest mainly Islam and Christianity

Major exports: tea, textiles and garments, rubber, coconut products, spices, gems

Major imports: petroleum, transport equipment, machinery, food and drink, textiles and clothing

Main destinations of exports: USA, UK, W. Germany, United Arab Emirates, Japan, Iraq, Pakistan

Main sources of imports: Japan, Saudi Arabia, Iran, UK, USA, Singapore, Malaysia, W. Germany

Capital: Sri Jayawardhanapura Kotte (founded 1982), an island 11 km east of Colombo. (Parliament and other government offices have been moved from Colombo.)

Government: constitutional democracy with President elected every six years

Head of State: President J.R. Jayawardene

Population: 16.1 million (1984), 2.1% annual growth rate in early 1980s
64% rural, 10% working on plantations, 26% urban
One of the highest population densities in Asia

Average life expectancy: 69 years

Infant mortality rate: 32 per 1000

Important historical dates/festivals celebrated:
February 4th – anniversary of independence from British rule (1948)
April – Sinhalese and Tamil New Year
Full moon day, May – Wesak, celebrating the birth, enlightenment and death of Lord Buddha
Late July/early August – Kandy Perahera and Vel festival
September 26th – Bandaranaike Commemoration Day (celebrating ex-Prime Minister Mrs Sirimavo Bandaranaike, who became the world's first woman Prime Minister in the mid-1960s)
Late October/early November – Hindu festival of Deepavali

International links: Sri Lanka is a member of the Commonwealth, the International Monetary Fund (IMF), the World Bank, the Asian Development Bank and the Colombo Plan, and a signatory of the GATT Trade Agreement. In 1983, Sri Lanka joined with six other countries on the Indian sub-continent to form the Organization for South Asian Regional Co-operation.

Index